Beetlejuice Beetlejuice Movie Review

The Real Story Behind the Movie

Miles Thatcher Publishing

Copyright

All rights reserved. No part of this book may be reproduced, stored in a retrieval system, or transmitted in any form or by any means, electronic, mechanical, photocopying, recording, or otherwise, without the prior written permission of the publisher, except for brief quotations used in reviews.

This book is a work of nonfiction. Any similarity to real persons, living or dead, is coincidental and not intended by the author.

Disclaimer

This review of *Beetlejuice Beetlejuice Movie Review: The Real Story Behind The Movie* is based on publicly available information, official announcements, and personal interpretations of the film's themes, characters, and production details. The content herein is intended for informative and entertainment purposes only. The review does not claim any insider knowledge, nor does it represent the opinions of the filmmakers, actors, or production companies involved in the film.

Any references to real-life events, historical facts, or other films are speculative and for contextual analysis. The review is not affiliated with Warner Bros., Tim Burton Productions, or any other entity associated with the production of *Beetlejuice Beetlejuice* (2024). Viewers are encouraged to watch the film and form their own opinions.

Table of Contents

Introduction

The world of *Beetlejuice* is unlike any other in film history. When Tim Burton introduced the impish, otherworldly character of Betelgeuse in 1988, audiences were attracted by his combination of dark humor, gothic flair, and wildly imaginative concept of the afterlife. More than three decades later, Burton has brought the odd bio-exorcist back to life in *Beetlejuice Beetlejuice* (2024), a widely anticipated sequel that revisits the unusual world of the dead with a contemporary twist.

In this review, we will go further into the 2024 film, providing new insights into the themes, people, and visual aspects that distinguish this sequel from the original. This is more than just a story about a prankster ghost; it is a film that delves into the distinctions between life and death, tradition and invention, humor and horror.

This book's chapter-by-chapter examination strives to present a detailed evaluation that delves below the surface, revealing the true tale behind *Beetlejuice Beetlejuice*. Whether you're a longtime admirer of the original or new to the universe of Betelgeuse, this review will provide an intriguing and fascinating look at one of the most anticipated films of 2024. Prepare to enter the afterlife as you have never seen it before.

Chapter One

Tim Burton's Vision – A Darkly Whimsical Revival

The 2024 sequel "Beetlejuice Beetlejuice" marks Tim Burton's return to the Beetlejuice universe, and it brilliantly captures the filmmaker's distinct blend of gothic, whimsical, and macabre storytelling. Burton, renowned for his unrivaled ability to combine the bizarre and charming, returns to the world of ghosts and ghouls. His vision, implemented with a heavy mix of dark humor and fanciful surrealism, breathes new life into the original 1988 hit while preserving its eccentric core.

The decision to revive Beetlejuice after more than three decades demonstrates the character's and Burton's everlasting appeal. The original Beetlejuice was a perfect storm of creative chaos—a plot that felt both disconnected and beautifully planned, owing to Burton's ability to transform the weird into the relatable. Burton's 2024 sequel retains that chaotic charm while also adding a new level of visual maturity. In this rendition, he dives deeper into issues like life, death, and the folly of existence, yet the overall tone is cheerful and lighthearted. His darkly whimsical resurrection of Beetlejuice feels like a celebration of the unusual and eccentric, as if asking people to bask in the grotesque beauty of his warped afterlife.

One of the most notable aspects of Burton's vision for the 2024 sequel is his use of set design and cinematography. In Beetlejuice Beetlejuice, the afterlife is more than just spooky ghosts; it is a fully fledged planet overflowing with life (ironically). From the warped buildings to the swirling hues that appear to defy science, Burton creates a visual feast that revels in the impossible. Every aspect of the afterlife in this picture feels like a journey into Burton's own imagination, a bizarre blend of the amusing and terrible. The meticulous attention to detail in these settings generates a distinct ambiance that is easily identifiable as Burton's work. The filmmaker's use of color, which alternates between subdued tones and brilliant bursts of life, heightens the contrast between the dullness of the living world and the bizarre brilliance of the afterlife.

Furthermore, Burton's fixation with combining the real and fantasy is on full display in Beetlejuice Beetlejuice. He's always been drawn to characters who don't quite fit in with society or reality. In this sequel, Lydia and her daughter Astrid are portrayed as outsiders caught up in the strangeness of the otherworldly. Lydia's goth aesthetic, which made her a cultural icon in the original, is now passed down to Astrid, albeit with a more rebellious modern edge. Burton brilliantly uses these people to reflect on how the world has evolved since 1988, and how the next generation approaches the macabre differently. While Lydia was marked by her morbid curiosity and melancholy reflection, Astrid introduces a more playful defiance, signifying a shift in tone that makes the film more accessible to new audiences while maintaining its nostalgic roots.

Of course, no discussion of Burton's vision is complete without mentioning Beetlejuice himself. Michael Keaton's portrayal of the wild, unashamedly incorrect ghost remains an important part of the film's success. Burton made the conscious decision not to soften Beetlejuice for current audiences. In fact, both Burton and Keaton appreciated Beetlejuice's politically incorrect, crass humor, claiming that his lack of character development is what made him so appealing. The character is not intended to change or be redeemed, but rather to stay as chaotic and obnoxious as ever. Burton's unwillingness to follow the present trend of character development is a bold move that harkens back to the anarchic spirit of the original film. Beetlejuice is not here to learn lessons; he is here to wreak havoc—and Burton lets him do so with unrestrained abandon.

Burton's reimagining of the Beetlejuice universe also offers new characters who blend effortlessly into his bizarre and eerie realm. Jenna Ortega's Astrid, for example, is an excellent modern companion to Lydia, both visually and philosophically. Whereas Lydia was a product of the late 1980s goth subculture, Astrid represents a new generation of kids who value uniqueness and rebellion, but with a modern twist. Burton's Astrid analyzes how the young outcast character has grown in today's environment while remaining connected to Lydia's legacy. Similarly, Monica Bellucci's character

Delores—Beetlejuice's ex-wife—provides a fascinating narrative for the titular ghost. Bellucci adds a sultry menace to the role, giving the film a slightly darker undertone that contrasts with the humor and demonstrating Burton's ability to balance the light and dark.

Burton's films are known for their balance of humor and horror, and Beetlejuice Beetlejuice exemplifies this. The picture is both funny and frightening at times. This paradox is part of what makes Burton's work so compelling: his ability to make the absurd seem regular and the monstrous feel familiar. Whether it's a horrific visual prank or a moment of slapstick comedy, Beetlejuice Beetlejuice's horror components never outweigh its humor, and vice versa. Instead, they work together to create a disturbing yet delightful viewing experience.

One of the most intriguing aspects of Burton's resurrection is his exploration of death and the afterlife. While the picture is clearly a comedy, there is an underlying meditation on mortality that runs throughout. In Burton's hands, death is not something to be feared, but something to be welcomed with levity and scorn. The afterlife in Beetlejuice Beetlejuice is portrayed not as a haven of peace or judgment, but as a bureaucratic nightmare populated by oddball spirits just trying to get by. This sarcastic take on death is a remark on the absurdity of existence, a concept that Burton has addressed in numerous films. In Beetlejuice Beetlejuice, he goes a step further, broadening the scope of the afterlife to make it feel like a live, breathing universe with its own set of rules and societal conventions.

The film also explores the topic of legacy, both via the characters and the film itself. Lydia's transformation from goth teen to mother parallels the history of the Beetlejuice franchise, which was once edgy and unorthodox but has now become part of pop culture's mainstream. However, Burton refuses to allow Beetlejuice Beetlejuice become a sterilized imitation of its former self. He retains the anarchic spirit of the original while adapting it for contemporary viewers. In doing so, he guarantees that Beetlejuice Beetlejuice is a relevant and compelling film in its own right, rather than a nostalgic throwback.

Finally, Burton's concept for Beetlejuice Beetlejuice is one of joyful defiance against the mundane. It's a film that encourages audiences to accept the weird, to laugh in the face of fear, and to see beauty in the unusual. His ability to create a universe that is both comical and macabre, where the dead are as alive as the living, is what makes his films so appealing. With Beetlejuice Beetlejuice, Burton demonstrates why he remains one of cinema's most distinctive voices—a filmmaker unafraid to explore the darker side of life while maintaining a sense of wonder and fun.

Chapter Two

The Evolution of Beetlejuice – Michael Keaton's Return

In 2024, Michael Keaton reprised the role of Betelgeuse, which he initially played in 1988 in Tim Burton's *Beetlejuice*, a film that became an immediate cult favorite. Keaton's performance in the original film was a career-defining event, cementing his reputation as a versatile actor capable of bringing dark comedy and wild unpredictability to life. With more than 30 years between his first performance and the 2024 sequel, Keaton's comeback is more than simply a nod to nostalgia; it's a testament to his ability to resurrect a character adored by many while remaining faithful to its core.

When *Beetlejuice* initially premiered in 1988, the movie was notable for its distinct blend of horror, comedy, and fantasy. At the time, Michael Keaton was well recognized for his work in comedies like *Mr. Mom* (1983) and *Night Shift* (1982). His performance as Betelgeuse was a dramatic departure from his previous performances, allowing him to explore a character who was equal parts hideous and charming, a force of chaos constrained by neither the rules of the living nor the dead. The original film's success—it grossed over $73 million at the box office and won the Academy Award for Best Makeup—established Betelgeuse as one of cinema's most distinctive and eccentric anti-heroes.

Fast forward to 2024, and Keaton's return to the character has been eagerly anticipated by fans who have long hoped for a sequel. The path to this picture, however, was long. Following the 1988 debut, there were several attempts to create a sequel, including the famously canceled *Beetlejuice Goes Hawaiian*, which was shelved after Keaton and Tim Burton got engaged with *Batman Returns* (1992). The ultimate announcement of *Beetlejuice Beetlejuice* in 2022 sparked enthusiasm among fans, and Keaton's return to the role has met those high expectations.

One of the most noticeable parts of Keaton's return is his flawless transition back into the role of Betelgeuse. Despite the three-decade difference, Keaton catches the anarchic spirit of the bio-exorcist, retaining all of his frenetic energy and irreverent humor. In an era when film sequels frequently emphasize character development and redemption arcs, Keaton's Betelgeuse defies tradition by remaining substantially unchanged. This was an intentional decision. In interviews, Tim Burton and Keaton discussed how Betelgeuse, as a character, did not need to mature or acquire new lessons. He exists outside moral limits, motivated simply by self-interest and chaos. Keaton welcomes this, presenting audiences with the same wild, unpredictable ghost that pleased and terrified them in 1988.

Keaton's performance combines physical comedy and verbal wit. His timing is superb, whether he's telling off-color jokes or breaking the fourth wall to interact with the audience. One of Betelgeuse's defining characteristics as a character is his unpredictability—viewers never know what he'll do or say next, which Keaton exploits to great effect in the sequel. His motions are frantic, his expressions exaggerated, and his mannerisms larger-than-life, all of which add to the chaotic energy that Betelgeuse delivers to every scene.

The improved visual effects in *Beetlejuice Beetlejuice* enable for even more innovative and original moments, yet Keaton keeps the character grounded throughout his performance. While CGI improves the otherworldly aspects of Betelgeuse's talents, Keaton's portrayal of the character truly brings him to life. The film's makeup and costume design, like the original, are critical in creating Betelgeuse's ugly yet charismatic image. The classic striped outfit has returned, as have the unkempt hair and deteriorating skin, cementing Keaton's return as a legitimate continuation of the character we first encountered decades ago.

The chemistry between Keaton and his co-stars is particularly noteworthy in the 2024 sequel. Winona Ryder, who returns as Lydia Deetz, now an adult and mother of a rebellious teenage daughter called Astrid (played by Jenna Ortega), has numerous notable confrontations with Keaton. Lydia's apprehension about Betelgeuse has been softened by the wisdom of age. Keaton and Ryder complement each other well, with Lydia now in greater control of the situation than she was when she was younger. However, Betelgeuse remains as wild as ever, wreaking havoc on Lydia's life once more, this time with her daughter involved.

Jenna Ortega's character, Astrid, adds a fresh dimension to the plot, and her encounters with Keaton's Betelgeuse are among the film's most hilarious. Astrid, like her mother in the original, is a rebellious girl who becomes fascinated with the afterlife and the mystical world that

Betelgeuse represents. Keaton's Betelgeuse instantly identifies Astrid's rebellious tendency and utilizes it to his advantage, influencing her in the same manner he once attempted to seduce Lydia. The generational shift in the Deetz family dynamic offers a new element to the sequel while remaining true to the original.

Keaton's return is further aided by Tim Burton's unrelenting devotion to keeping the whimsical, gothic atmosphere that marked the original *Beetlejuice*. Betelgeuse's universe is as weird and visually striking as ever, with Burton's distinctive use of contrasting colors, deformed buildings, and surreal landscapes creating a fanciful and slightly ominous atmosphere. Keaton's Betelgeuse flourishes in this environment, his crazy personality complementing the odd sights.

As much as the film relies on humor and absurdity, there are moments of deep meditation, notably on the themes of death and the hereafter. In the original film, Betelgeuse was a character who resided between the living and the dead, manipulating the rules of both realms to his advantage. In the 2024 sequel, Keaton's Betelgeuse continues to play this job, but there is a sense that time has passed in the afterlife. While Betelgeuse remains mostly unchanged, the world around him has changed, and Keaton's acting reflects the subtle shift in tone.

The film's climax shows Keaton at his best, combining humor, chaos, and a hint of menace.

Betelgeuse's pranks approach a climax as he orchestrates a slew of extraordinary happenings that threaten to upend both the living and the dead. Keaton's ability to shift between funny and somber moments keeps the viewer guessing, never knowing what to expect next. His depiction exemplifies why Betelgeuse has remained a popular figure for almost three decades: he is surprising, funny, and completely unforgettable.

Chapter Three

Lydia Deetz – The Gothic Queen Grows Up

In *Beetlejuice Beetlejuice* (2024), Winona Ryder reprises her classic role as Lydia Deetz, but this time she brings with her a lifetime of adventures in both the human and spirit realms. Lydia was the typical goth teen, symbolizing disenchantment with the normal society with her gloomy attire, pale face, and deadpan looks. She was a symbol of countercultural cool, disconnected but full of emotion that struck a chord with viewers.

In this new edition, Lydia Deetz has matured from a rebellious teen to a mother with her own complicated life. This move comes as a surprise to many who remember her as the girl who almost married Beetlejuice to save her ghostly buddies. Lydia's development is viewed as a natural progression, but it preserves continuity, keeping her the same cherished character.

Lydia is shown in the film as a lady managing the problems of parenthood while being tied to the creepy world of the uncanny. Her daughter, Astrid, played by Jenna Ortega, has Lydia's rebellious nature, resulting in an intriguing mother-daughter dynamic that drives the film's emotional center. Lydia's problem is not just dealing with her adolescent daughter, but also reconciling her past and present. Living in a world still haunted by Beetlejuice, Lydia must choose between fulfilling her responsibilities as a mother and safeguarding her daughter from the very perils she once flirted with.

Winona Ryder's performance as Lydia captures the character of a woman who has matured while maintaining the dark sensibility that distinguished her earlier self. Her character is no longer just a passive witness of the strange world around her. She has evolved into an active participant who understands the supernatural world better than any other character. This awareness enables her to handle the tumultuous events that occur when her daughter, Astrid, discovers an old model of the town in the attic, sparking a fresh series of uncanny events.

Lydia's performance in *Beetlejuice Beetlejuice* (2024) is also distinguished by her efforts to safeguard her family while dealing with her continuing link to the underworld. Astrid discovers facts about Lydia's history, the link between mother and daughter is tested. Lydia's attempt to keep Beetlejuice at away is a physical, emotional, and psychological battle. As the film progresses, we witness Alice plagued not just by the real ghost of Beetlejuice, but also by the metaphorical ghosts of her previous decisions and unresolved difficulties.

Lydia's encounter with her daughter exemplifies the generational shift in how they perceive the supernatural. Lydia was once the moody youngster lured to the macabre, but now she's attempting to keep her daughter from falling into the same traps. Lydia's dual role as protector and as someone who previously needed protection creates a deep emotional arc that contrasts with her somewhat static character in the original film. She has grown into a character that blends her caustic wit and acute intelligence with real care for her child, demonstrating how even the most unusual characters may change in sympathetic ways.

The film does not hide the reality that Lydia, despite her maturation, remains intimately attached to the peculiarities of her surroundings. Her exchanges with her stepmother, Delia Deetz (played again by Catherine O'Hara), provide moments of levity and nostalgia. Delia, who is now presenting an art show in London, is as odd as ever, and her difficult but love connection with Lydia serves as a reminder that even in the strangest situations, family relationships endure. Delia's colorful personality and new job in the arts stand in stark contrast to Lydia's grounded yet magical presence, emphasizing the Deetz family's constant tension between the conventional and otherworldly.

One of the film's most intriguing components is Lydia's emotional condition, which reflects her surroundings. Lydia's obligations have weighed heavily on the previously bright and hopeful attitude of the Deetz household. The original's wonderfully whimsical tones remain, but they are matched with a greater depth of emotion reflecting Lydia's psychological difficulties. Her home, once a unique safe haven for ghosts and people alike, now houses memories of both joy and grief. The film's set design and visual choices gently reflect Lydia's journey—her home is packed with eclectic art and bizarre antiques, but it also feels lived-in, symbolizing her endeavor to merge two worlds.

Ryder's acting as Lydia is particularly effective in the quiet moments when she focuses on her history. These passages allow the audience to perceive Lydia as more than just the goth icon of their memories, but also as a woman who has faced terrible decisions. The significance of her decisions, particularly her encounters with Beetlejuice, becomes obvious as the film goes. These moments are packed with subtle emotion as Lydia is forced to confront the truth that her past acts may come back to haunt her in ways she never imagined.

Lydia's journey in *Beetlejuice Beetlejuice* (2024) is intriguing because it feels organic. She is not a caricature of her past self, but a fully developed character who has evolved alongside the audience. Her humor, which was earlier tinged with cynicism and detachment, now has a stronger sense of irony. Her wit remains sharp, but it is softened by the knowledge that comes with age and experience. Ryder's ability to balance Lydia's multiple layers of personality makes her return to the part both nostalgic and refreshing.

Lydia's position as both mother and mediator between the living and the dead becomes increasingly important as the film progresses to its conclusion. The mystical qualities that formerly captivated Lydia are now a serious threat to her family, pushing Lydia to face Beetlejuice head on. Lydia's strength in this new conflict comes from her grasp of both realms. She knows how to navigate the strange laws of the afterlife, but she also recognizes the value of human connection. This duality makes her an interesting character in the sequel, as she fights not just for her daughter's safety, but also for her family's future.

Chapter Four

Introducing Astrid – The New Deetz Prodigy

Astrid Deetz, the new character in *Beetlejuice Beetlejuice* (2024), is more than a rebellious adolescent; she serves as a link between the Deetz family's two generations and the chaotic world of Beetlejuice. Astrid, played by Jenna Ortega, brings new life into the brand with her feisty independence, quick wit, and natural curiosity, all of which resemble her mother, Lydia Deetz. Whereas Lydia was the quintessential goth teen in the 1988 version, Astrid represents a new generation of teens—rebellious yet far more knowledgeable about the supernatural world. This juxtaposition lends depth to the film's narrative, elevating it above a repetition of previous cliches.

One of Astrid's most compelling traits is her ability to handle the difficulties of her relationship with her mother, Lydia, while still establishing her own path. Lydia, who was previously haunted by Beetlejuice, is now attempting to protect her daughter from the evils of the afterlife. However, in classic adolescent form, Astrid is lured to the very things her mother cautions her of. This disobedience is motivated by more than simply defiance; it derives from her natural curiosity and desire to understand the realm beyond the living. She is captivated by the strange model of the town concealed in the attic, a relic from her mother's history that serves as the key to reopening the door to the afterlife. Astrid is a character who is both wary and enthralled, divided between her mother's caution and her own longing for adventure.

Ortega's portrayal of Astrid is nothing short of captivating. She adds an edge to the character, making her both approachable and surprising. While Lydia in the original film was known for her melancholy demeanor and isolation from the world around her, Astrid is more energetic and aggressive. She refuses to remain a passive observer; instead, she takes action. This contrast is significant because it emphasizes the age difference between the two characters. Lydia's gothic detachment echoed the tone of the late 1980s, a period when teenage angst and apathy were prevalent in popular culture. Astrid, on the other hand, exemplifies the modern teen: socially conscious, inquisitive, and reluctant to sit on the sidelines.

The mother-daughter relationship between Astrid and Lydia adds another emotional element to the drama. Lydia's care for her daughter is apparent, but she is also haunted by unresolved traumas from previous interactions with Beetlejuice. Lydia sees Astrid as a younger version of herself, which scares and irritates her. The tension between them is more than simply usual teenage rebellion; it stems from Lydia's concern that Astrid would fall into the same traps that nearly caught her years ago. This complicates and multi-dimensionalizes their connection, as both characters try to defend each other from the supernatural forces that threaten to disrupt their lives.

The discovery of the mystery model in the attic, which represents the divide between the living and the dead, is essential to Astrid's plot. This model, which played an important role in the original film, serves as the spark for Astrid's journey to the afterlife. Unlike her mother, who discovered the supernatural by chance, Astrid's quest is planned. She seeks out the unknown, motivated by both curiosity and a sense of destiny. This makes her persona more proactive and adventurous than her mother, distinguishing her as a new type of heroine in the franchise.

Astrid's bond with Beetlejuice is yet another intriguing part of her character. While Lydia was originally turned off by Beetlejuice's filthy humor and unusual demeanor, Astrid is more attracted by him. She sees him not just as a ghost, but as a possible ally in her search for answers. This dynamic creates an intriguing tension between them, as Beetlejuice, who feeds on disorder, sees a kindred spirit in Astrid. He attempts to control her, as he did with Lydia, but Astrid is far more astute and resistant to his schemes. This sparks a peculiar power struggle between the two, with Astrid refusing to be a pawn in Beetlejuice's plans.

Ortega's connection with Michael Keaton is explosive, and their scenes together are bursting with energy. While Keaton's Beetlejuice is as irreverent and unpredictable as ever, Astrid's no-nonsense demeanor keeps him under control.

She isn't intimidated by him, which makes their encounters even more hilarious. In many respects, Astrid is the ideal counterpoint for Beetlejuice since she refuses to let him rule her while also not being afraid to use him to achieve her own aims. This dynamic adds a new level of complexity to the film, since the audience never knows whether Astrid is being influenced by Beetlejuice or if she is pulling the strings.

Astrid's part in the film emphasizes the topic of generational heritage. She inherited the Deetz family's link to the supernatural, but she treats it in a far different manner than her mother. Whereas Lydia was afraid and hesitant to confront the afterlife, Astrid is eager to do so. This shift in attitude reflects the shifting cultural landscape, in which younger generations are more willing to discuss taboo topics such as death and the afterlife. Astrid's persona exemplifies this transition, making her a modern heroine who isn't scared to face the unknown.

One of Astrid's most appealing characteristics is her unpredictable nature. She's more than just a rebellious teenager; she's a multifaceted character with her own goals and desires. At times, she appears to be siding with Beetlejuice, but then she backs off, demonstrating a stronger moral compass than the audience might assume. This uncertainty puts the viewers on edge since they never know where Astrid's quest will lead. Will she succumb to the pandemonium of the afterlife, or will she find a way to outwit Beetlejuice and save her family?

In many ways, Astrid's persona represents the modern generation's relationship with the past. She feels emotionally connected to her family's heritage, but she is equally determined to forge her own path. This makes her character immensely sympathetic, as many young people today struggle with the conflict between following history and establishing their own identities. Astrid's trip is about more than just exploring the afterlife; it's about discovering her position in the world, both as a Deetz and as a person. This paradox makes her one of the film's most interesting characters and a fitting successor to Lydia's legacy.

Chapter Five

Supporting Cast – The Oddballs and Ghostly Entities

In 'Beetlejuice Beetlejuice' (2024), the supporting cast provides a dynamic mix of weird individuals and ghostly creatures that add to the film's unusual tone. The picture, directed by Tim Burton, combines dark comedy and fantastical aspects, which is represented in the diverse cast of characters beyond the title character. Each supporting character adds layers of intricacy to the story, embellishing the otherworldly realm of *Beetlejuice* with remarkable performances that find a balance between absurdity and depth.

Monica Bellucci has a remarkable performance as Delores, Beetlejuice's ex-wife. Delores is a soul-sucking witch who poisoned Beetlejuice during the Black Plague centuries ago, prompting him to slay her with an axe. Bellucci's performance of Delores adds a sensuous threat to the film, creating an unnerving but curiously sensual atmosphere. Her history with Beetlejuice introduces a subtext of long-held grievances and a gothic romantic element to the story. Bellucci portrays Delores' mysterious and dangerous attraction, making her an enemy as well as a tragic person. Delores' encounters with Beetlejuice are tense, infused with dark comedy, and evocative of the stormy relationships that define Burton's characters. Her ability to shift between otherworldly terror and vulnerability makes her an essential aspect of the plot, adding to the mythology of the *Beetlejuice* universe.

Willem Dafoe also shines as Wolf Jackson, a ghost detective and former B-movie action star. In life, Wolf was known for his over-the-top performances in low-budget horror films, and after death, he uses that same enthusiasm to solve otherworldly riddles. Dafoe's performance adds a sense of campy pleasure to the film, as he fully embraces his character's idiosyncrasies. His exaggerated gestures and melodramatic delivery are suited for the film's odd tone. Wolf Jackson's character pays homage to traditional detective noir cliches, but with a paranormal twist. His performance as a ghost detective researching other ghostly phenomena provides a fascinating depth of intrigue to the picture, complimenting the main action while also standing alone as a quirky subplot. Dafoe's portrayal gives comedic relief, but underlying the humor is a character struggling with his identity in the afterlife, matching the philosophical issues frequently explored in Burton's films.

Catherine O'Hara reprises her role as Lydia's stepmother, Delia Deetz, from the original *Beetlejuice. Delia is now a well-known art curator, having hosted a famous art display in London's Soho district. O'Hara's comedic timing is still spot on, and she breathes new life into Delia's character. While Delia's infatuation with avant-garde art and status persists, her character has grown and evolved. She's no longer just an eccentric artist; she's a widow dealing with her stepdaughter's strange life choices and the lingering shadow of Beetlejuice. O'Hara's portrayal is both funny and touching, capturing the ridiculousness of her character's life while anchoring it in genuine emotions. Delia's relationships with Lydia and Astrid depict a strained but loving family dynamic, which adds emotional depth to the film's unusual story. The juxtaposition between Delia's high-society manner and the otherworldly pandemonium surrounding her fuels much of the film's humor.

Justin Theroux portrays Rory, Lydia's current boyfriend and television producer. Although Theroux's character is grounded in the real world, he is dragged into the otherworldly mayhem that surrounds Lydia and her family. As a television producer, Rory is obsessed with sensational stories, and his interest in the Deetz family's ghostly encounters drives much of the film's conflict. Theroux portrays Rory as both ambitious and suspicious, providing a counterpoint to the film's magical themes. His conversations with Beetlejuice and other ghostly creatures frequently expose his more cynical side, providing a grounded viewpoint amidst the otherworldly silliness. Despite his cynicism, Rory is eventually dragged into the lunacy of the afterlife, and Theroux's nuanced acting serves to balance the humorous and emotional parts of his character.

Jenna Ortega also plays Astrid Deetz, a crucial supporting character. Astrid, Lydia's teenage daughter, embodies her mother's rebellious spirit from the original *Beetlejuice*. Ortega's performance as Astrid is both charming and edgy, making her a key role in the film's plot. She discovers the model town in the attic, which triggers a series of supernatural events that reintroduce Beetlejuice into the Deetz family's lives. Astrid's curiosity and boldness make her an engaging heroine in her own right, and her interaction with Beetlejuice is one of the film's high points. Ortega portrays Astrid with an ideal balance of adolescent disobedience and tenderness, giving her character emotional depth that contrasts with the hilarious pandemonium around her. Lydia and Astrid's generational connections make for an intriguing narrative thread, as both women navigate the fuzzy line between the living and the dead.

Danny DeVito has a brief but noteworthy performance as the unidentified janitor, a ghost who committed suicide by swallowing varnish. DeVito's character, however minor, represents the film's dark comedy. His tragic history is played for laughs, but DeVito imbues his character with a caustic wit that heightens the film's macabre appeal. The janitor's appearance in the hereafter serves as a reminder of the film's investigation of death and what lies beyond, but his interactions with Beetlejuice and the Deetz family are played for comedic effect, ensuring that the picture never gets overly dark.

Chapter Six

The Humor, Horror, and Fantasy Mix

The 2024 *Beetlejuice Beetlejuice* film takes a daring approach by combining humor, horror, and fantasy, retaining the quirky appeal that made the original a cult favorite while adding levels of complexity. This exquisite blend of genres reflects director Tim Burton's distinct cinematic vision and Michael Keaton's legendary depiction of Beetlejuice. The film's charm stems from its capacity to make audiences laugh, cringe, and wonder at its magical features all in one sequence. This subchapter delves into how the film manages to combine these seemingly divergent components, generating an emotional rollercoaster that keeps viewers engaged from beginning to end.

One of the film's main qualities is its seamless crossover between humor and horror. In many films, both genres battle, with one overshadowing the other, but here they coexist to the point of symbiosis. Beetlejuice is the pinnacle of this blend, with his irreverent comedy, vulgar jokes, and crazy actions frequently juxtaposed with very scary scenes. For example, his capacity to summon animals from the afterlife or affect the living world produces events that could be terrible, but his smart one-liners and careless attitude turn them into amusing situations. This delicate balance is what makes Beetlejuice such a memorable figure, and Keaton's portrayal highlights this duality. Whether he's telling death jokes or terrorizing the living with his antics, Keaton keeps the audience guessing whether to laugh or scream.

The film's humor is generally dark, focusing on macabre themes that are both disturbing and humorous. Tim Burton's unique gothic aesthetic pervades the film, creating an environment in which the hideous becomes hilarious. The afterlife, for example, is portrayed as a bureaucratic nightmare, with infinite waiting rooms and illogical laws. Ghosts waiting to be processed, shrunken heads, and other strange figures fill this universe, making death a source of humor rather than horror. This satirical take on the afterlife is one of the film's most effective comedy components, as it challenges conventional wisdom about what happens after death. Rather than a serious voyage into the unknown, the afterlife in *Beetlejuice* is chaotic, inefficient, and full of amusing anomalies. Burton's ability to bring humor into death-related themes allows the picture to tackle serious topics without becoming overly weighty or dismal.

At the same time, *Beetlejuice Beetlejuice* embraces horror, especially in its visual components. The film's combination of real effects, stop-motion animation, and creepy set designs creates a disturbing atmosphere that contrasts dramatically with its comedic tone. Scenes in which Beetlejuice morphs into monstrous monsters or when the dead return to engage with the living cause anxiety. The film avoids jump scares and gore, instead using its distinct design to create an eerie world in which everything is possible. The town model in the attic, for example, functions as both a charming set piece and a portal to the afterlife, with its small houses and roads setting the stage for some of the film's most horrific scenes. These moments demonstrate the balance of humor and terror, with the imaginative and horrific coexisting together.

Fantasy plays an important role in *Beetlejuice Beetlejuice*, bringing both the horror and the hilarity to new heights. The picture is unconstrained by the boundaries of reality, allowing it to explore bizarre and innovative notions that keep the audience wondering. The supernatural components of the story—ghosts, afterlife regions, and magical powers—are all handled with awe and imagination. Burton's ability to create a world in which the dead walk among the living without hesitation lends the film an otherworldly quality, which adds to its appeal. This fantasy-driven approach allows for some of the most innovative and memorable scenes in the picture, including Beetlejuice's transformations, the living-dead dinner party, and the strange animals that inhabit the hereafter. These features are not only visually appealing, but also contribute to the film's humor and horror, making the magical world both alluring and horrifying.

The film's ability to sustain suspense while still making people chuckle is a tribute to its superb storyline and direction. The story's rhythm ensures that tension-filled scenes are regularly broken up by humor, keeping the picture from becoming too gloomy or overwhelming. The comedy timing is flawless, with Beetlejuice's bizarre behavior providing comic relief at precisely the appropriate times. At the same time, the horror components are never overshadowed by the humor; they coexist in a way that lets both flourish. For example, Beetlejuice's attempt to marry Lydia Deetz is both ludicrous and disturbing. His vulgar quips about marriage are amusing, but the underlying threat of his behavior puts the audience on edge, displaying how the picture navigates the delicate line between comedy and horror.

One of the most engaging aspects of Beetlejuice. Beetlejuice* is known for its unpredictability. The film's blend of genres keeps the audience guessing, as it seamlessly transitions from laugh-out-loud moments to frightening situations. This unpredictability is an important part of what makes the film so entertaining—it never lets the spectator become too comfortable. Just when you think you're seeing a lighthearted comedy, the picture throws in a genuine horror scene, reminding you that Beetlejuice's world is as dangerous as it is hilarious. This continual shift in tone keeps viewers on their toes and ensures that there are no dull moments.

The supporting characters help to maintain the film's balance of humor, horror, and fantasy. Lydia Deetz, played by Winona Ryder, is a steadying force in the middle of the pandemonium, and her goth demeanor adds to the film's dark humor. Her exchanges with Beetlejuice are among the film's most memorable scenes, as her deadpan answers to his outlandish conduct emphasize the absurdity of the scenario. Similarly, Jenna Ortega's portrayal of Astrid adds a new energy to the picture, with her rebellious nature echoing Lydia's younger self and providing new dynamics. The supporting cast of ghosts, monsters, and other supernatural beings contribute to the film's fantasy aspects, with each character bringing their own distinct brand of humor or terror to the scene.

Chapter Seven

Beetlejuice's World – The Afterlife Like You've Never Seen It

In *Beetlejuice Beetlejuice* (2024), Tim Burton once again transports audiences to the bizarre, eccentric, and darkly amusing world of the afterlife, a realm beyond our imagination. The afterlife in this picture is not simply a continuation of what audiences saw in the first *Beetlejuice* (1988), but rather a bright, vibrant development of it. As we follow Lydia Deetz's rebellious teenage daughter, Astrid, on her escapades, we discover new and unusual facets of this otherworldly realm.

From the time Astrid discovers the model of Winter River in the attic—a relic that once connected Beetlejuice to the living world—the film transports viewers to a depiction of the afterlife that feels more weird, surreal, and alive than ever before. This time, it's more than just Beetlejuice's trickery or the bizarre bureaucracy of the undead; it's an investigation of totally new regions that call conventional assumptions about life after death into question.

One of the most notable characteristics of the 2024 film is the refinement of the afterlife style, which reflects Tim Burton's development as a director. The picture successfully blends the familiar with the unexpected, preserving some of the original film's goofy, grotesque charm while incorporating darker, more cerebral undertones. The afterlife is shown as a chaotic tangle of layers and levels, each with its own set of rules.

The physical degradation of the protagonists in the afterlife contrasts sharply with the unusual beauty of their surroundings.

Burton's typical use of contrasting colors—bright neons against shadowy backdrops—gives the afterlife a weird, dreamy feel. In this world, nothing is ever quite as it appears, with strange animals lurking in the corners, objects behaving in unexpected ways, and an ever-present sensation that reality is changeable. The continual sense of surprise keeps Astrid and the audience on edge. The end result is an environment that is alive with possibilities and danger, resulting in a captivating and visually appealing narrative.

The afterlife's extension is both visual and thematic. In *Beetlejuice Beetlejuice*, the afterlife serves as a metaphor for unsolved concerns, for things that don't quite fit into either the living or the dead worlds. Astrid's accidental opening of the doorway to this realm implies that past mistakes, unsolved trauma, and lingering emotions all leave echoes that last after death. In this way, the afterlife is more than just a setting for the story; it is a dynamic entity that responds to the protagonists' emotional states and decisions.

One of the most intriguing new elements in the film is the introduction of the "Lost Souls Room," a location that plays a far larger role than it did in the original. Here, we witness the spirits of individuals who were unable to find peace in death and are now caught in limbo, neither entirely living nor completely dead. The chamber is a chilling reminder of the dangers of not confronting one's own personal problems. It reflects the characters' internal conflicts, particularly Astrid's, as she fights with her sense of self, her problematic connection with her mother, and Beetlejuice's rising impact in her life.

The film also reveals new locations in the afterlife, such as the strange "Dimension of Doors," a region where one can visit any number of different worlds via a series of elaborate, ominous doorways. Each door opens into a different, unforeseen universe, suggesting the unlimited possibilities of what follows after death and, more broadly, the infinite choices we face in life. Astrid's trip through this maze of doors serves as a metaphor for her coming of age, as she learns to traverse the complexity of the real and unreal.

Beetlejuice's status as a trickster is emphasized in this segment. He manipulates the fundamental fabric of the afterlife, changing the rules to suit his needs. In one scenario, he literally rearranges elements of the afterlife like game pieces, demonstrating his power and chaos. Despite his pranks, Beetlejuice remains a figure of pathos—a spirit stuck in the world he rules. His ambition to escape to the living world and cause havoc derives from his dissatisfaction with the afterlife, giving him a more complicated character than a one-dimensional evil.

Lydia Deetz, now older and wiser, has a more contemplative role in the film. Her encounters with the afterlife, both in the original film and now as a mother, give her a unique perspective on its complexities. She has come to realize that death, in this universe, is a change, a state in which one's unfinished business must be completed. Lydia's character journey adds emotional weight to the picture as she guides her daughter through the maze world of the afterlife, all while dealing with her own lingering worries and regrets.

As the story progresses, we see the living and dead collide in increasingly tangible ways. The walls between the two worlds get weaker, allowing for more direct interaction between the characters from each realm. The film uses this collision not only as a plot device, but also as a statement on how the past, present, and future are interrelated. The afterlife, as shown in *Beetlejuice Beetlejuice*, is a world where time appears to bend and twist, allowing for moments of contemplation, sorrow, and, ultimately, redemption.

One of the film's most riveting scenes is Astrid's encounter with Delores, Beetlejuice's spiteful ex-wife who lives in a dark area of the afterlife. Delores represents the darker side of the world, driven by hatred and a thirst for vengeance. Her presence acts as a warning that the hereafter is not a perfect place; unresolved emotions can fester and become harmful. Delores' interactions with Astrid and Lydia heighten the film's intensity, as they must confront not only the supernatural perils of the afterlife, but also the emotional scars left by the past.

The 2024 version of *Beetlejuice Beetlejuice* further expands the scope of what the afterlife can symbolize. While the first film depicted it as a bureaucratic nightmare full of humor and absurdity, the second further explores its philosophical implications. The idea that the afterlife reflects our choices in life becomes a key issue. Astrid's quest is about more than just avoiding the ghosts of the past; it's also about comprehending how her current decisions will impact her future.

Made in the USA
Las Vegas, NV
29 November 2024

12908506R00039